ACORN RAIN

poems by

Francey Jo Grossman Kennedy

Finishing Line Press
Georgetown, Kentucky

ACORN RAIN

Copyright © 2020 by Francey Jo Grossman Kennedy
ISBN 978-1-64662-241-2 First Edition
All rights reserved under International and Pan-American Copyright Conventions. No part of this book may be reproduced in any manner whatsoever without written permission from the publisher, except in the case of brief quotations embodied in critical articles and reviews.

ACKNOWLEDGMENTS

Grateful acknowledgement to these journals for first publishing the following poems:

Momentary Stay appeared in *Stars in Our Hearts: Whispers*, World Poetry Movement. ed. Hilary Clark, 2011.
Millennium Moon: Solar Eclipse appeared in *Poetry of the Golden Generation*, Volume V, 2010, Kennesaw State University.
Acorn Rain appeared in *Poetry of the Golden Generation*, Volume IV, 2008, Kennesaw State University.
Apples Cupcakes and Beige appeared in *JAEPL Journal of the Assembly for Expanded Perspectives on Learning*, Volume III, 1997.
Old Smokey's Warning appeared in *Georgia State Review*, Fall 1996.
Stockings appeared in *Georgia State University Review*, Spring 1995.
Sky Puzzle appeared in *Georgia State University Review*, Winter 1994.

With deep gratitude I thank Marie Howe for her fearless honesty, gentle guidance and faithful encouragement.

I thank the dear pilgrims of our brave Ireland and Italy writing circle.

I thank with sincere appreciation Ivana Mestrovic and Meghan Adler, for generous close reading.

I forever thank Steve Jaffe for his steady heart and willing presence.

I thank Amy, Holly, and Francey for their love and inspiration.

Publisher: Leah Maines
Editor: Christen Kincaid
Cover Art: Francey Jo Grossman Kennedy
Author Photo: Austin Martin
Cover Design: Elizabeth Maines McCleavy

Order online: www.finishinglinepress.com
also available on amazon.com

Author inquiries and mail orders:
Finishing Line Press
P. O. Box 1626
Georgetown, Kentucky 40324
U. S. A.

Table of Contents

Momentary Stay 1
No Curfew/No Violets 2
Millennium Moon: Lunar Eclipse 3

Momma Fixed Grits for Yankees 5
Sherman's Marching Song 7
When You Sat at the Kitchen Table 8
She Told Her Children—Go Away 9
Apples Cupcakes and Beige 10
Sky Puzzle 12

August Green 14
Old Smokey's Warning 15
Stockings 16
Dandelion Wine 17
Union Leader's Daughter 18
My Father Loved Piano Music 19

December Real Baby 21
Rock a Bye Brother Mine 22
Golden Oldies 23
Black and White and Gray 24
Heart Shaped 25
Brother Loved the Big Woods 26

Irish Father on St. Patrick's Day 27
Family's Silent Night 28

Where Have You Been 30
Acorn Rain 32

Acorn Rain honors the memory of
Grandma Fanny Lee Canada
Dad and Momma
Brother Ron

What is spoken is never, and in no language, what is said.
Martin Heidegger from Poetry, Language, Thought

Let us dare to have solitude—to face the eternal, to find others,
to see ourselves. —Paul Tillich from *The Eternal Now*

Momentary Stay

How deep does river of memory flow
      in any moment's hour
ever shifting from yesterday's
      too bright shallow

to unfathomable depths,
      where voiceless hidden cruelty
      is falsely buried
      with no bidding to return.

Who would not have half-told narratives
      and uninvited shadows stilled
      but for a momentary stay—

I beg you
      for a fragment of the sunrise.

No Curfew/No Violets

Then   I listened
to hear a voice
calling me home.

We had no curfew
running the streets barefoot,
toes covered, gray fine silt and alley cinders
no time to "come in" from the dark

playing Kick the Can and Fox Release the Den
in the neighborhood
serious crimes were ringing a false fire alarm,
stealing candy bars, and taking turns posturing bully.

We raced the block between the beer garden
and the back door of the Italian restaurant.
I loved watching the neon light
turn on to sanitize the toilet seat
in the ladies' bathroom on the corner gas station,

all before condoms were required to say "Hello"
in that world of fragmented faith
childhood's willing suspension of dis-trust.

Rain rainier rainiest relentless
puddles of mud
where the flowers grew last spring;
I have learned not to expect a rose garden
but I confess
I had still hoped to see the colors of wild flowers.

My posture is unchanged
here I stand—
Why then does the ground feel so close
that my face scratches the dirt

and my crying waters the earth
     where the violets used to grow.

Millennium Moon: Lunar Eclipse

Wearing my brother's old Viet Nam Marine
full dress coat, olive fine wool, moth eaten at the hem,
I dance in the dark,
watching semi circles
spheres swinging wider and wider into dark shadows
around earth's new millennium moon.

Startled sensibilities in the planet's revolution
Time's turning—the whole world must be told.
Call a night crier   awake a lamplighter
Come see the sky.

No minor chill of zero
measures this unmistakable trembling
See Look Watch
Old millennium solstice gone,
low horizon tangible globe of December.

But Here Now—*Oh Look*
Oh Oh Look and See
we are the children of long ago,
before mandated kindergarten time.
We met Dick and Jane
Puff and Spot, yellow raincoats, splashing puddles,
all together in locked down desks
bolted seats called first grade.

We drew circles; we made spirals
we knew the difference between Sun and Moon,
Night and Day, Cold and Dark.
Now in this new night
Call the world.
If not, Call *all allie, allie in free.*

Keep a vigil with me
Dance me under the stars
say I'm not dreaming in the moon's ephemeral black night
tell me I am awake
tell me each and each and each are here—*breathing*
in this improbable search for a terrestrial domain
safe, only whole—when holding you.

Momma Fixed Grits for Yankees

Momma filled old black iron trays
    corn bread sticks
    heavier black iron skillets
    yellow rounds cut in triangles dripped with molasses
    she called corn bread cake

Momma peeled apples for pies
    twisted her hands in old cloths until
    her fingers and palms were
    purple —dyed in grape juice

    picked black berries
    sewed crazy quilts (was anyone sane?)
    sewed yellow checked sundresses
    hung the wash on the line with her homemade clothes pole
    talked of *her people*
    called them on holidays or when somebody died
    handed the telephone to each, one by one to say, Hello.

Nobody told us
that in the country of *her people*
they drawled, "Hey" instead of a two syllable "Hello"
Nobody told her
little black balls would be comin' through the window
dancing on the winter window sills—soot balls
from Pennsylvania's steel mills
instead of Alabama's red farm dirt and

Momma kept on cookin' grits for her six babies
So *Hush, you' all.*
Don't tell her of the cold
Don't tell her, *Put your shoes on*
Don't tell anyone—we buried her in Yankee Land
and maybe
Momma will never guess those ain't magnolia trees
but will reckon
she is with *her people.*
We left her dreamin' in her sleep
after we sang "The Old Rugged Cross" and
as we turned from that place
I'm sure I heard someone whisper,
    I reckon I'll be fixin' grits today.

Sherman's Marching Song

In seventh grade chorus we practiced
"America the Beautiful," "You're A Grand Old Flag" all verses,
and certainly, "My Country 'Tis of Thee."

Our proud Yankee heritage
patriotic hymns and robust songs
included the Union General's marching song:

> *"Sherman's dashing Yankee boys*
> *Will never reach the coast*
> *So the saucy rebels said . . .*
> *Had they ever thought to reckon with the host?"*

all so long ago
pictures in our history books, kind of like fiction
so we didn't know the real story
behind our unwelcome chants,

singing loudly to our Alabama Mama
harsh songs of the defeated South
the proud southern faith
once held promises.

Hearing our raucous words
a country bride
in smoky steel town western Pennsylvania
maybe, still grieving for her own mama's
homemade corn bread
fried okra with black eyed peas,

some tall Yankee had already
broken several promises to her.

We wondered whether her sadness
pondering a return to *her people*
    would be a song
        of victory or defeat.

When You Sat at the Kitchen Table

Some kitchen table tales forgotten
some more slowly dim.

You told stories of red dirt and azealas
daffodil blooms in early Spring

of Aunt Sadie Belle
coming North to land of cold
to be in February snow
birth time of your first daughter.

Next added second daughter's birth,
naming another sister Aunt Ozelle
riding the train from Alabama
(blessedly it was Spring).

Then you gave us Biddy's name
arriving for the birth of your first son

I do remember second brother
hospital born December twenty-fourth
my six year old crying Christmas morning
'cause Mama was missing

and indelibly remember third baby boy
born on my eleventh birthday
proudly mine—gift for me,

"but wait a minute, Mama," third daughter cries
you left something out
who came when I was born?
        "Oh, I reckon I never told them about you."

She Told Her Children—Go Away

I do not want you here
she told her grown sons and daughters
by her bedside
we did not listen

changes once barely perceptible
withered to inescapable vulnerabilities
reminding her of last winter's crippling—

dreaded incapacity's stark black—
wheel chair still in far corner
she calls any attention: condescension

wants no Florence Nightingale
seeks no angel to break this spell
shrieks *leave me alone*
we did not listen

Samaritans and Tennessee's Blanche
tout a blessing: "always depend on
the kindness of strangers"
message to her blood brood "*unwanted*"

eager faces, generous gestures uninvited.
hospitality for hope unwelcome
this wonted refuge seeks only solitude's
avowed offer: benign neglect

she tells us when we go away
come whispers from those no longer here

had we been silent or wakeful
maybe we, too, would have heard
we did not listen.

Apples Cupcakes and Beige

When body's buried grief is recognized
in light of language
it can be named—

Saturday regular bus trips downtown
mother's weekly errands meant a single
red apple for me.
Seventh grade lunches included waxed paper
rewrapped cupcakes.

Mother's color was beige—blouses, shoes,
dresses, coats. I loved yellow and blue.
Mother sewed my Christmas pageant dress
on her busy Singer—brown velvet.

Camus's stranger alleged he did not know
which day his mother died.
I know exactly—September Labor Day.

October, November, December submerged in fog —
by the end of January
blurred back to awareness,
I began buying apples
green, golden, granny, heart shaped,
red delicious prize quality 'til the full
refrigerator overflowed.
I did not eat any.

I bought chocolate Twinkies filled with cream
wrapped in clear cellophane, many many packages
and more, and ate the cakes all at once.
I bought an ugly beige corduroy jacket
wore it every day.

Finally, I awoke in the middle of the night
screaming I am not a dying frail old woman.

I burned the jacket
the chocolate crusade is over
and
a day came when I saw a tiny little brown bird
nondescript, as they say, and
I am not as afraid of Spring as I was

Sky Puzzle

If ever the Winter sky
again turns
and surely surely
it will,
memory holds that
piece of bright blue
missing in this hour,
but clearly shaped
to fit an empty patch.

I always hated
lost puzzle pieces
especially the noticeable sky.

Old dark green shrubs,
some obscurity near
the flat bottom frame
maybe no one would notice,
but the sky missing
is too much.
To want to complete the picture,
yet throwing out the whole earth
because of a patch of sky
has not been found acceptable.

Will the eye
learn to see what is Not there
tracing invisible patterns
and choosing inner colors?

Blue is not the only sky hue
perhaps
the fill-in-the-gap
allows
color me black, purple, bruised
color me light.
No one really ever lost the sky,
just the eye's capacity
to see so far,
when brave puzzlers
have always known
you don't need every piece
to see the picture.

August Green

I still hear Daddy's words,
Your skin heals before it is cut.
I questioned his sayings with, "No"
"Not so," "How could that be?"

He knew broken skin begins to heal
before the wound bleeds,
something about epidermis and cells.
His dictums I carry daily
assured he taught of body's hidden powers.

August's dense stillness speaks Autumn in the air
Leaves darker than Summer green
indelibly blotched, and seasoned past

Spring's pale blossoming
    of transparent whimsy, faint hue
    more the fairytale shimmer
    of far away castles —not truly real
but *surely seen* from blinking distance.

Leaves of deepest green announce
yellow much too soon will come
shaking trees bare
with wind and cold and dark.

I once dreaded the season called death,
now see invisible shapes
on bare waving limbs
in November's shadows,
    palest gold of Spring's imperceptible color.

Wounds are healed
    by mysteries lived
    before the bleeding begins.

Old Smokey's Warning

A barking dog
awakens me from deep
into now
with no boundaries from here to there.

The dog barks me
to another broken sleep
when my bedroom open window
overlooked the moonlit backyard
and old brown-gray Smokey
howled at lightning
or warned of strangers in the alley.

Untroubled by old Smokey,
head on pillow,
I'd wait
to hear Daddy's ritual shouting
from the little bathroom window.
His yelling failed to silence the dog
but ever quieted me,
hearing all players in place.

Barking dogs in the night
in the now
another domain
of other boundaries

no shouts are heard
only the quiet

where silence howls.

Stockings

Back then
The stockings were real
gray with red toes
and white cuffs
and longer than long,
hung by the fireplace
      to hold
         an orange
         an apple
         a walnut
         a candy cane,
what else I cannot recall.

Except
they were real,
worn and washed,
dried on a line
with wooden pins,
not artificial red
trimmed in synthetic cotton
where no one can place
a foot
or toe.
You let us hang your real woolen socks.

Sometimes,
under the night sky
      I hear
         your real voice
         your real words
         your real laughter,
telling me   *now*,
      you know where to place your foot.

Dandelion Wine

The lettering on the envelope
distinctly yours, deliberate, original—
as no other writes, created, practiced,
adopted as a boy, you told me,
a script I once sought to imitate.

Tall, dark, you wore boots, carried a metal lunch box
knew magical formulas for dandelion wine,
caramel corn, meatloaf recipes,
shoe polishes, nosegays, oils for rifle barrels.

Following along beside you across bridges,
I climbed a cement ledge—a balance beam,
over rushing water, holding tight to your hand—fearless.

Another day, quietly still in a mission pew,
I heard you speak
in a meeting for tired people who need *steps*.

You listened to my dining room piano practice
"Beautiful Dreamer" or "Paderewski's Minuet"
from the darkened living room, catching any missing note.

Today I hold an empty envelope, a discovery yielded
from the bottom of desk drawer depths;
the date tells the year, the month, before all letters stopped.

I search memory for a hint of the past enclosed message,
something original, no doubt,
made with dark molasses and raw honey.

I know no key to the mystery of missing contents
until seeing again through blurred re-vision
your distinctive hand, has carefully scripted
a name in print, not mine—
      a letter to my own little daughter
      who asks,
      Where is Grandpa? Is he making dandelion wine?

Union Leader's Daughter

Breathing trembles in chilling battle un-declared
my temples beat until vision blurs
elsewhere is my true passion,

yet, if I fail to stand resolute in this assault
no future clash will erase this proving ground
where I surrendered.

Second grade encounters—Oak Street Elementary School
I wore puffed sleeved cotton dresses
sashes untied by Frankie and Mike.

Once Gibby stole my sash, wore as banner
on ball field playground,
my indignant cries revealing joy, " He chose me."

While teasing was child's play
the hungry men gathered on the front porch
making signs, empty metal lunch boxes home,

heavy oiled boots in silent closets
with power to call *Strike*.
Work stopped. Stalled. I knew them to be giants.

My father fought hard—gladiator, strongest mediator
unrepentant he paid the price.

I carry no slingshot but wage battle
with the unnamed invisible. I know only
this has fallen to me—

to engage faceless phantoms
who know nothing of a proud history

but dogged enough to lower their eyes
refusing reflection in mirrors of shame.

My Father Loved Piano Music

When my father chose the red haired
high-tempered woman
known for her teaching excellence
to give me piano lessons,
I was eight.

My father loved piano music.
He listened to my practicing
on an old upright,
Pederowski's Minuet—
from the darkened living room,
called out when I missed a note.

He tied a black silk bow
on my cast
the year I fell and broke my arm
and could only play with one hand.

My father loved piano music.
My teacher's tantrums grew more intense
during the three years of lessons.
She screamed, Count!
insisting I deliberately did not listen.
My tears enraged her.

One day, arriving for my lesson
I told her, "I am not coming back."
I walked home slowly,
a long walk
through dangerous parts of the city.

My father loved piano music.
He yelled, "You will practice twice as long every day."
This demand faded—
the piano was long silent.

Then—I saw in a small room
off the formal reception area
in my college dormitory
a baby grand piano.
I played between classes and in the evening.

On a weekend break, I returned home
My piano was gone—missing.
"Where is my piano?"
"Dad sold it. He said no one played it."

Mother watched in silence
as I searched for my portfolio
and stacks of sheet music
"Where's my music?"
Beethoven, Mozart, Hayden?
Finally, she said, "It's lost."
My little brother told me,
"Dad burned your music in the furnace."

My father loved piano music.

December Real Baby
for Thomas John

That Christmas Eve I still believed in Santa Claus.
I think so . . . yes I did.
Not the Christmas our oldest sister secretly led
us to the locked attic cupboard to disclose a
delinquent discovery—
sleds, a bicycle, treasures from Toyland.

Momma's hurting disappointment, learning we knew
made us sad and wondering. She did not cry.
No—that holiday, my six year old Christmas,
I cried, *Momma is not here.*

Between early bed time 'cause Santa's coming and
early morning, Momma 's gone missing.
My gift, a wooden table with chairs, just my size,
was no consolation.

Three days later she brought a different present
baby brother brown eyes (like mine) brown curls,
round, a real baby—Thomas John now the littlest one.
I loved him.
First hair cut, barber shop—his curls gone, I cried.

He was the most beautiful two years old. Why else
could I have been so uncaring? jealous ?
Where was I when he called from a high shelf?
The question abides.

He cried. I did not rescue him. He fell. Broken leg
         (believed by no one that I put him there).
Then he became even more adorable—little boy
running fast with a cast.

He grew strong, brave, and boldly dared to rescue others.

Many years later when I told him of my still guilt,
his tender words added measure to long needed healing,
         "Sis, my leg healed years ago.
                 You were just a little girl."

Rock a Bye Brother Mine
for James Edward

Rock a bye baby in the tree tops
beautiful little brother grown I once
held rocking singing you
three months old into sleepy baby time.

When the wind blows . . .
Just after your safe arrival, a thrombosis heart
attacks Father, then hospital Daddy
for interminable months "Will he live through this night?"

He lived—with scary coronary threats again—again.
Mother stressed—distressed twisting hair
into little knots, eyes faraway Mama—
haunted ghosts came to abide in her eyes

five brothers and sisters told not to cry.
I took your picture dressed in silk pink ribbons, my baby dress,
pretending I have a little sister.
No little sister could have become my hero then

when the bough breaks
to be here through sun's and star's indescribable losses.

volunteering to live for God and country in Nam's Hell
foxholes with buddies' bodies blown to bits,
spit on in Marine uniform by *peace* lovers
to guard the men laboring for steel, vigilante for safety
to choose bold words in cold grease mill of work night, and day,
with mid-turns backwards in battles of stupidity,

to plant cedar trees
to speak softly to a six-year-old little girl
to rescue a wild baby kitten
to build a cross for a grave
    to Rock   to sing
                when the wind blows
                when the cradle rocks
                when the bough breaks
                when down comes.

Golden Oldies on June 6th

Golden Oldies "I'll Be Seeing You"
"Good Night Sweetheart"
Public Broadcasting plays in celebration

I aloof stay until
the announcer calls out Big Band Era
who danced to Glenn Miller?

Not next door young woman Thelma
two brothers in formal Army khaki sharp
framed pictures posted in the window
why keep a living room so dark?

Born World War II baby, uncomprehending
air raids lights out, blinds pulled,
newsreels D-Day—cheers, confetti parade
why grown-ups tears still weeping?

Years since passed, battle movies galore
I watch many landings on Omaha Beach
keep remembering my brother there—
when we all know *his* war

was combat veteran's spit upon return.
Belated and recent recognition
barely begun:
Hate the War/ Love the Soldier

Keep hearing June sixth songs?
can words bring some
a little closer to each brother on the beach
when reconciliation—when healing comes.

Black and White and Gray
for Ronald Perry

In the photograph—
you, my brother, and I the same height
stand side by side—*smiling*
next to spindly purple spider plants,
reaching as tall as our shoulders.
Our background, Mama's flower garden,
tirelessly recreated year by year
in the small triangle of dirt near the back porch.

Maybe—we are eight and seven or nine and eight years old.
I do not remember.

Black and white photography
does not reveal
the apricot color of my short silk dress
nor does the angle
show the sash tied in a big bow behind my back
You wear a front button shirt, tucked in short pants.

The grays of the picture—or memory
offer no clue to the hue of your clothing;
surely, even in Kodak living color, the camera could not
have captured those blue eyes.

In take-my-picture posture, facing forward
slightly turned toward each other,
we hold our arms bent
wearing full size boxing gloves
in false opponent's stance.

You—my strongest advocate ever.
I was never mad at you

                      until you smashed your head
against that tree around the curve on the icy road
where no gloves could save you.

Heart Shaped

Robin egg blue,
wide heart shaped back window
Dad's 1950's vehicle—Kaiser

only little brother called, "Go Kaisey"
five older siblings remembered
going any where meant *walking*

We knew the *why*
of the transformation to transportation—
a matter of the heart.

Decade of Eisenhower's time
coronary patients prescribed bed-rest
months, long hospital captivity
urgent restrictions.

Dad lived and loved driving the blue Kaiser
baby brother grew up to own a truck
just like Dad's new truck,
just like both brothers.

No one knew three sons
each carried
a weak heart gene or damaged valve

whatever mysterious coronary fragility
inherited from the car owner
with the heart shaped window.

Kaiser production did not last long
neither did the *first*
of the Silverado brothers.

Brother Loved the Big Woods

Ron's driving
Ice
Hit the tree
Instant out
Surely newspaper details
What vehicle?
I read the report
Quickly put away
Only
February cold
Cold phone call

And they told me
later
two younger sons
traveled one hundred miles North
to the Big Woods
Not to hunt
       God's creatures
              but to bury a brother.

Irish Father's Marks on Saint Patrick's Day

long ago
ancient fathers broke terror of thunder
storms and sun's hiding,
declaring scientific explanations
sufficient to erase
delusional fantasies
questions of why

my Celtic father in less faraway moment
told me:
> *If I get there first, I'll make a mark.*
> *If you get there first, erase it.*
sounding absolute authority

such instruction translated strange
even to an eight year old, more
strange—why no pursuit, no debate?
deliberate, he was undeniably protective
in those heedfully blind years—

years marked by perceptible confusion
gentle good night songs and prayers
blurring broken glass, smashed mirrors
leather strap threats
some promises kept

can any erasing of chaotic care
keep cherished memory safe

Family's Silent Night

Once upon a time
my blue eyed sister
with long golden hair
fair skin
said, *"No Sir"*
refusing to walk *up* the stairs
so he could knock
her back *down*—

he screamed at her;
she ran away
from the top step,
past the second landing
around the corner
not seen from the first landing
where the wooden post
held the pretty little white church
music box,
mother securely taped
every Christmas
to play "Silent Night."

We went to church—
that much is sure
Sunday meatloaf and potatoes
told to be quiet
Momma planted morning glories
purple spider plants, and petunias.

Daddy oiled his guns
hunted in the big woods
until his heart cried "enough"
smoked cigarettes in a hospital room
after I obeyed his request
turn off the oxygen tank
and stand guard outside the door.

One sister ran away, *again*
another sister tried to take care
of every—thing.

I read another book
my little eight year old brother
was arrested for breaking
the mean old neighbor's fish pond

I watched
police officers drive him away
seated alone
in the backseat of the patrol car.

Where Have You Been?

Where have you been?
    In the desert

How was the world there?
    Strangely weary, abject in suspended lull
    quite black until I grew used to the barrenness

Were you frightened?
    Sometimes   then I surrendered

What were you most afraid of?
    Memories—too many
    uninvited, vivid sad inextinguishable

So what now?
    I do not know   only I see differently
    now I do know
    my house was on fire and my children did burn.

What else did you learn?
    watched the dogwood tree blossom
    then the storms came,
    the rain pounded the white petals to the ground.

    saw Spring come to the brown January world
    where silhouetted trees made stick figures against
    the changing morning sky

    I fell asleep praying: God—Remember my name
    Night after night
    I woke up crying   daylight hurt my eyes

I asked God
> tell each and each of the missing (gone to heaven's home)
> or hidden in earth's paralysis
> tell them, " I love you."

And then
> I mailed an April birthday gift
> And forgave as many in heaven and earth as I could on any one day.

Acorn Rain

The acorns fell that year
in late October, early November
like hail stones spinning on the roof
loud, disconcerting, prodigious, singular.

Still, I rather liked the sounds
once recognized
the rhythm's warm beat—acorn rain,
Not ice storm's reckless brutality,

following weeks, weeks into months'
mission waiting for rude death's halt
with deep hope of *might—maybe—perhaps*
this indelible mark assigned elsewhere, or at least
an extension for the final
futility reigned—

until the brown waves of winter grass
came into focus
in the shine of rotting leaves.

Once raked, task completed, the dismal ground
revealed hidden tiny pale green wings
buried acorns
engendered in the dark, earth protected

baby trees—rooted
imperiled,
radiant, unbound unexpected,
whispering, *Present.*

F**rancey Jo Grossman Kennedy** from Western Pennsylvania, with Yankee Dad and Alabama Momma (her bi-lingual claim) is named for her Grandmother Fanny Lee Canada.

Awarded the Ph.D. from Emory University's Graduate Institute of Liberal Arts Interdisciplinary Program, she studied Psychology/ Literature. Slippery Rock University her Alma Mater was first appointment teaching Composition/ Literature; other teaching includes Georgia State University, and Creative Writing Oglethorpe University.

Her writing appears in *Georgia State University Review, Kennesaw State University Golden Series, Adanna, Artemis,* among other publications. Studying with mentor Marie Howe in Italy and Ireland with fellow writers is significant to her poetry.

She is the third daughter of a third daughter and has three daughters Amy and Holly and Francey—each ever an inspiration to her.

Loving Beethoven and Chopin, she plays piano for Emory University Winship Institute's volunteer Arts Program.

Her black Chow-chow Epiphany (Eppy) keeps her company. Francey Jo loves the ocean and paints the sky.

www.ingramcontent.com/pod-product-compliance
Lightning Source LLC
LaVergne TN
LVHW041559070426
835507LV00011B/1189